## Hello, Family Members,

Learning to read is one of the most important accomplishments of early childhood. **Hello Reader!** books are designed to help children become skilled readers who like to read. Beginning readers learn to read by remembering frequently used words like "the," "is," and "and"; by using phonics skills to decode new words; and by interpreting picture and text clues. These books provide both the stories children enjoy and the structure they need to read fluently and independently. Here are suggestions for helping your child *before*, *during*, and *after* reading:

### Before
- Look at the cover and pictures and have your child predict what the story is about.
- Read the story to your child.
- Encourage your child to chime in with familiar words and phrases.
- Echo read with your child by reading a line first and having your child read it after you do.

### During
- Have your child think about a word he or she does not recognize right away. Provide hints such as "Let's see if we know the sounds" and "Have we read other words like this one?"
- Encourage your child to use phonics skills to sound out new words.
- Provide the word for your child when more assistance is needed so that he or she does not struggle and the experience of reading with you is a positive one.
- Encourage your child to have fun by reading with a lot of expression...like an actor!

### After
- Have your child keep lists of interesting and favorite words.
- Encourage your child to read the books over and over again. Have him or her read to brothers, sisters, grandparents, and even teddy bears. Repeated readings develop confidence in young readers.
- Talk about the stories. Ask and answer questions. Share ideas about the funniest and most interesting characters and events in the stories.

I do hope that you and your child enjoy this book.

—Francie Alexander
Chief Education Officer,
Scholastic Education

*For Nina Irene,*
*my little honeybee.*
*— J.E.G.*

*For Craig,*
*my sweetest valentine.*
*— P.B.*

Text copyright © 2003 by Jane E. Gerver.
Illustrations copyright © 2003 by Priscilla Burris.
All rights reserved.  Published by Scholastic Inc.
SCHOLASTIC, CARTWHEEL BOOKS, and associated logos are trademarks
and/or registered trademarks of Scholastic Inc.

Library of Congress Cataloging-in-Publication Data
Gerver, Jane E.
  The sweetest valentines / by Jane E. Gerver ; illustrated by Priscilla Burris.
    p. cm. — (Hello reader)
Summary: Fred uses unconventional methods to make valentines for all his friends, with very satisfactory results.
  ISBN 0-439-28308-6
  [1. Valentine's Day — Fiction. 2. Stories in rhyme.]  I. Burris, Priscilla, ill. II. Title. III. Series.
  PZ8.3.G3275 Sw 2003
  [E]--dc21                                                                 2002006029)

10  9  8  7  6  5  4  3  2                              03  04  05  06  07

Printed in the U.S.A. 24 • First printing, January 2003

# The Sweetest Valentines

by Jane E. Gerver
Illustrated by Priscilla Burris

Hello Reader! — Level 1

SCHOLASTIC INC. Cartwheel ·B·O·O·K·S·®
New York   Toronto   London   Auckland   Sydney
Mexico City   New Delhi   Hong Kong   Buenos Aires

Tomorrow will be Valentine's Day!

The class is making cards.

Here are paper, lace, and glue.

Fred says, "This won't be hard!"

Will Fred use paper that is red
or paper that is pink?

Which color will look best with lace?

Fred thinks and thinks and thinks.

Sue cuts out a lot of hearts.

She pastes them one by one.

Jean draws a
pretty garden.

Jack draws a
yellow sun.

Ray cuts out a cupid

and a bow and arrow, too.

Fred gets to work.

He cuts and draws.

Oh, no—

there goes the glue!

"Time to stop!" Fred's teacher says.

Her name is Mrs. Fox.

But Fred does not have any cards

to drop into the box.

All his friends are going home.

Fred follows. He feels mad.

"I did not make my valentines!"

Now Fred is feeling sad.

Fred walks through the forest,

past Jean, Jack, Ray, and Sue.

And then Fred gets a bright idea!

He knows just what to do.

Fred eats his dinner.

He takes his bath.

He gets to work—and then...

he gets a little messy...

and needs a bath again!

Valentine's Day is here at last!
Mrs. Fox stands in the crowd.
Each student picks a valentine
and reads the name aloud.

Jean gets a card from her friend Jack.

Ray gets a card from Sue.

And Fred gives cards to everyone.
"For you...and you...and you!

"I hope you like these valentines.
I made them by myself!
There was no more lace or glitter
or paper on the shelf.

"I made hearts from leaves and
feathers.
And I used some acorns, too.
I stuck them on with honey,
since I had no paste or glue."

Sue's valentine
is the reddest.

And Ray's card
is the neatest.

Jean's heart
is the biggest.

But Fred's cards are the sweetest!

Fred gives a valentine to his mom.

She asks, "Is this for me?

Thank you so much, my little Fred—

you are my honeybee!"